Colorful Blessings Deluxe

Moments of GRACE

A COLORING BOOK OF FAITHFUL EXPRESSION

The LORD is my **Shepherd**
Psalm 23:1

ILLUSTRATIONS BY PATRICIA HILL

ST. MARTIN'S GRIFFIN

NEW YORK

For no word from God will ever fail.

Luke 1:37

The Lord is my strength and song . . .

Psalm 118:14

For I am not ashamed of the gospel, because it is the power of God that brings salvation to everyone who believes.

Romans 1:16

On days when I am afraid,
I put my trust in you.

Psalm 56:3

"I am the way, and the truth, and the life."

John 14:6

God is spirit, and those who worship
him must worship in spirit and truth.

John 4:24

Faith . . .

It's not about knowing
what the future holds,
but knowing
who holds the future.

Now faith is the assurance of things hoped
for, the conviction of things not seen.

Hebrews 11:1

The LORD is the strength of his people ...

Psalm 28:8

WHEN LIFE KNOCKS YOU DOWN, ROLL OVER AND LOOK AT THE STARS.

The heavens declare the glory of God; the skies proclaim the work of his hands.

Psalm 19:1

As a mother comforts her child,
so I will comfort you . . .

Isaiah 66:13

And the Lord direct your hearts into the love of God, and into the patient waiting for Christ.

2 Thessalonians 3:5

LOVE

Love is patient,
love is kind.
It does not envy, it does not boast, it is not proud.
It does not dishonor others, it is
not self-seeking, it is not
easily angered, it keeps
no record of wrongs. Love
does not delight in evil but
rejoices with the truth.
It always protects,
always trusts,
always hopes,
always perseveres.

LOVE never fails.

1 Corinthians 13:4–8

Mine eyes are ever toward the LORD . . .

Psalm 25:15

You have given me the shield of
your salvation, and your right hand
has supported me; your help
has made me great.

Psalm 18:35–36

If God
is for us,
who can be
against us?

Romans 8:31

Remain alert. Keep standing firm
in your faith. Keep on being
courageous and strong.

1 Corinthians 16:13

For we walk by *faith*, not by *sight*.

2 Corinthians 5:7

Awake, my glory! Awake, O harp
and lyre! I will awake the dawn!

Psalm 57:8

Shake yourself from the dust; ARISE!

Isaiah 52:2

Depart from evil, and do good;
seek peace, and pursue it.

Psalm 34:14

Delight yourself in the LORD;
And He will give you the
desires of your heart.

Psalm 37:4

Rejoice always!

1 Thessalonians 5:16

Fearing any human being is a trap,
but confiding in the Lord
keeps anyone safe.

Proverbs 29:25

Even though I walk through the valley of the shadow of death, I will fear no evil, for you are with me; your rod and your staff, they comfort me.

Psalm 23:4

For God did not send his Son into the
world to condemn the world; but that
the world through him might be saved.

John 3:17

"No one comes to the Father except through me. If you had known me, you would have known my Father also."

John 14:6–7

Many are the plans in the mind of a man,
but it is the purpose of the Lord that will stand.

Proverbs 19:21

The future is BRIGHT!

"For I know the plans that I have for you," declares the LORD, "plans for well-being, and not for calamity, in order to give you a future and a hope."

Jeremiah 29:11

The LORD gives strength unto his people;
the LORD will bless his people with peace.

Psalm 29:11

"I have the right to do anything," you say—but not everything is beneficial. "I have the right to do anything"—but not everything is constructive.

1 Corinthians 10:23

THE TEN COMMANDMENTS

I
I AM THE LORD THY GOD
THOU SHALT HAVE NO OTHER
GODS BEFORE ME.

II
THOU SHALT NOT MAKE UNTO
THEE ANY GRAVEN IMAGE

III
THOU SHALT NOT TAKE THE NAME
OF THE LORD THY GOD IN VAIN

IV
REMEMBER THE SABBATH DAY,
TO KEEP IT HOLY.

V
HONOUR THY FATHER
AND THY MOTHER

VI
THOU SHALT NOT KILL.

VII
THOU SHALT NOT COMMIT ADULTERY.

VIII
THOU SHALT NOT STEAL.

IX
THOU SHALT NOT BEAR FALSE
WITNESS AGAINST THY NEIGHBOUR.

X
THOU SHALT NOT COVET

EXODUS 20:1–17

When I said, My foot slippeth;
thy mercy, O Lord, held me up.

Psalm 94:18

Worry less ...

Pray more!

Do not be anxious about anything, but in every situation, by prayer and petition, with thanksgiving, present your requests to God. And the peace of God, which transcends all understanding, will guard your hearts and your minds in Christ Jesus.

Philippians 4:6–7

Let the words of my mouth, and the
meditation of my heart, be acceptable
in thy sight, O Lord, my strength,
and my redeemer.

Psalm 19:14

The LORD is near to all who call upon him,
To all who call on Him in truth.

Psalm 145:18

Those who trust in the LORD
will renew their strength;
they will soar on wings like eagles;
they will run and not grow weary;
they will walk and not faint.

Isaiah 40:31

With all my heart I have sought You;
Do not let me wander from
Your commandments.

Psalm 119:10

The name of the LORD is a strong tower; The righteous runs into it and is safe.

Proverbs 18:10

And walk in love, as Christ loved us
and gave himself up for us, a fragrant
offering and sacrifice to God.

Ephesians 5:2

"For God so loved the world, that he gave his only Son, that whoever believes in him should not perish but have eternal life."

John 3:16

Then you will call upon me and come
and pray to me, and I will hear you.

Jeremiah 29:12

"Ask, and it will be given to you; seek, and you will find; knock, and it will be opened to you."

Matthew 7:7

For the Son of Man has come to seek
and to save that which was lost.

Luke 19:10

For I am sure that
neither death nor life,
nor angels nor rulers . . .
will be able to separate
us from the love of God
in Christ Jesus
our Lord.

Romans 8:38–39

I will proclaim the name of the Lord.
Oh, praise the greatness of our God!

Deuteronomy 32:3

Sing to the
LORD,
all the earth.
Proclaim His
salvation from
day to day.

I Chronicles 16:23

Let the peace of Christ rule in your hearts.

Colossians 3:15

"I have told you this so that through me you may have peace. In the world you'll have trouble, but be courageous—I've overcome the world!"

John 16:33

The grace of the Lord Jesus Christ
be with your spirit. Amen.

Philemon 1:25

G God's

R Riches

A at

C Christ's

E Expense

The LORD is near to the brokenhearted
And saves those who are crushed in spirit.

Psalm 34:18

Have I not commanded you?

Be strong
and courageous.

Do not be afraid;
do not be discouraged,
for the Lord your God will
be with you wherever you go.

Joshua 1:9

For everyone who has been born of
God overcomes the world. And this
is the victory that has overcome the
world—our faith.

1 John 5:4

THE JOY OF THE LORD IS YOUR STRENGTH

Nehemiah 8:10

O give thanks to the LORD,
call upon his name;
make known his deeds
among the peoples!

Psalm 105:1

Rejoice
in the
LORD
always.
I will say it again:
Rejoice!

Philippians 4:4

I have chosen the way of faithfulness;
I set your rules before me.

Psalm 119:30

If you OBEY my voice and keep my covenant you shall be my treasured possession out of all the peoples.

Exodus 19:5

For thy loving kindness is before mine eyes:
and I have walked in thy truth.

Psalm 26:3

And the Word became flesh, and dwelt among us, and we saw His glory, glory as of the only begotten from the Father, full of grace and truth.

John 1:14

Every man's way is right in his own eyes,
But the LORD weighs the hearts.

Proverbs 21:2

Fruits of the Spirit

Love

Joy

Peace

Patience

Kindness

Goodness

Faithfulness

Gentleness

SELF-CONTROL

Against such thing there is no law.
Galatians 5:22–23

But seek first the kingdom of God and his righteousness, and all these things will be added to you.

Matthew 6:33

And let us not grow weary of doing good, for in due season we will reap, if we do not give up.

Galatians 6:9

Before the mountains were formed
or the earth and the world
were brought forth, you are God
from eternity to eternity.

Psalm 90:2

You are the light of the world.

Matthew 5:14

Good and upright is the LORD: therefore
will he teach sinners in the way.

Psalm 25:8

For all have sinned and fall short of the glory of God, and all are justified freely by his grace through the redemption that came by Christ Jesus.

Romans 3:23

I will instruct you and teach you in the
way you should go; I will counsel you
with my eye upon you.

Psalm 32:8

Trust in the LORD
with all your heart
and lean not on your
own understanding;
in all your ways
acknowledge him,
and he will make
your paths straight.

Proverbs 3:5–6

For every house is built by someone,
but the builder of all things is God.

Hebrews 3:4

He has made everything beautiful in its time.

Ecclesiastes 3:11

I wait for the LORD; my soul waits,
and I will hope in his word.

Psalm 130:5

What is impossible with man
is possible with God.

Luke 18:27

Behold, how good and pleasant it is
when brothers dwell in unity!

Psalm 133:1

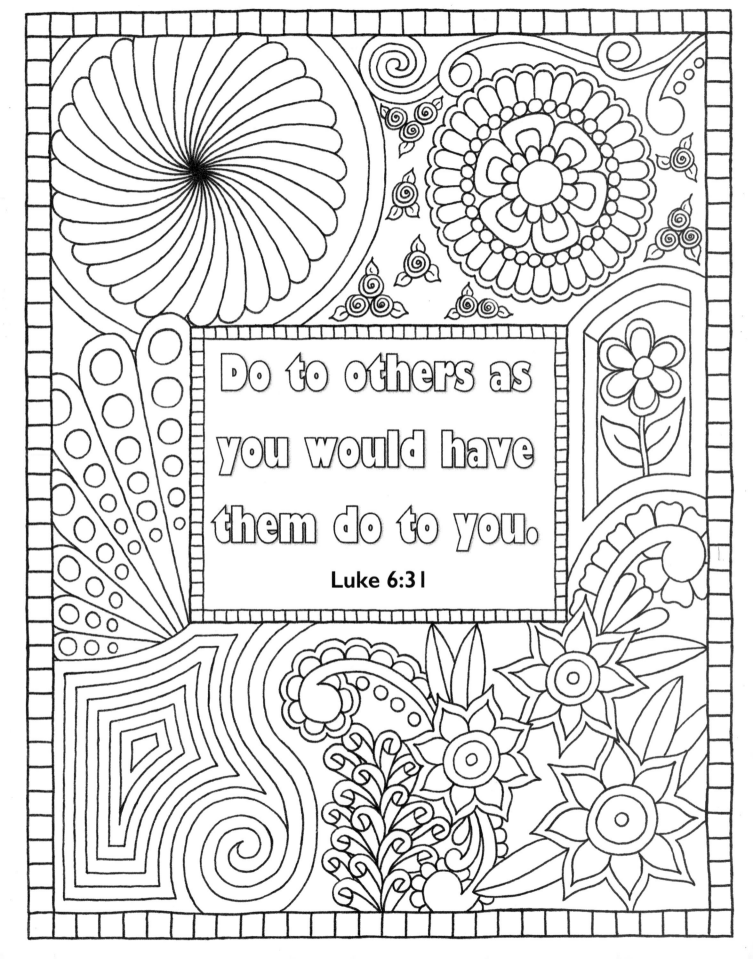

Do to others as you would have them do to you.

Luke 6:31

I am the vine; you are the branches.

John 15:5

Give thanks to the LORD, for he is good; his love endures forever.

1 Chronicles 16:34

I am at rest in God alone; my salvation
comes from Him.

Psalm 62:1

For it is by grace you have been saved, through faith— and this is not from yourselves, it is the gift of God— not by works, so that no one can boast.

Ephesians 2:8–9

For who is God, but the LORD?
And who is a rock, except our God?

Psalm 18:31

Cast all your

anxiety

on him because

he cares for you.

1 Peter 5:7

And those who know your name put
their trust in you, for you, O LORD,
have not forsaken those who seek you.

Psalm 9:10

So, whether you eat or drink, or whatever you do, do all to the glory of God.

1 Corinthians 10:31

All day long he continues to crave,
while the righteous person gives
without holding back.

Proverbs 21:26

Death and life are in
the power of the tongue,
And those who love it
will eat its fruit.

Proverbs 18:21

God is love, and the one who
abides in love abides in God,
and God abides in him.

1 John 4:16

Beloved, let us love
one another,
for love is from God;
and everyone who
loves is born of God
and knows God.

1 John 4:7

How much better is it
to get wisdom than gold!

Proverbs 16:16

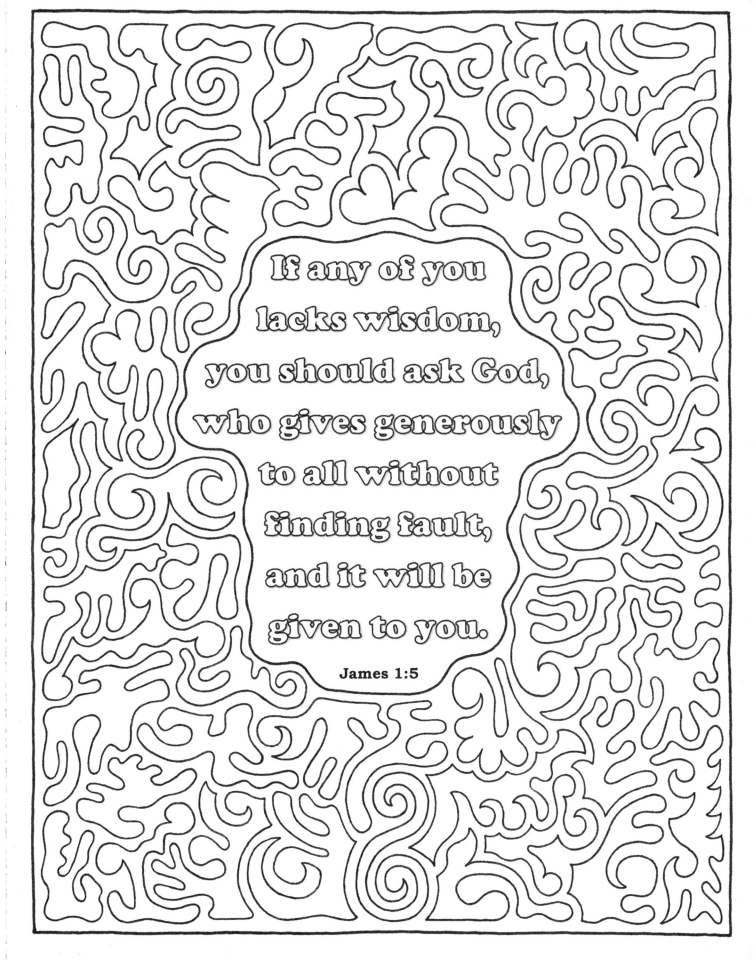

If any of you lacks wisdom, you should ask God, who gives generously to all without finding fault, and it will be given to you.

James 1:5

Fear not, little flock; for it is
your Father's good pleasure
to give you the kingdom.

Luke 12:32

Whoever gives thought to the word
will discover good, and blessed is he
who trusts in the LORD.

Proverbs 16:20

Blessed are the pure in heart, for they will see God.

Matthew 5:8

GOD, the Lord, is my strength;
he makes my feet like the deer's;
he makes me tread on my high places.

Habakkuk 3:19

Mercy unto you, and peace, and love,
be multiplied.

Jude 1:2

And God is able to bless you abundantly, so that in all things at all times, having all that you need, you will abound in every good work.

2 Corinthians 9:8

But be doers of the word, and not
hearers only, deceiving yourselves.

James 1:22

"It is written,
'Man shall not live
by bread alone,
but by every word
that comes from
the mouth of God.'"

Matthew 4:4

For whatever is born of God overcomes
the world; and this is the victory that has
overcome the world—our faith.

1 John 5:4

"If you have faith
like a grain of mustard seed,
you will say to this mountain,
'Move from here to there,'
and it will move,
and nothing will be
impossible for you."

Matthew 17:20

Make every effort to keep the unity
of the Spirit through the bond of peace.

Ephesians 4:3

Bear one another's burdens, and thereby
fulfill the law of Christ.

Galatians 6:2

One thing I have asked from
the LORD, that I shall seek:
That I may dwell in the house
of the LORD all the days of my life,
To behold the beauty of the LORD
And to meditate in His temple.

Psalm 27:4

COME NEAR TO GOD AND HE WILL COME NEAR TO YOU.

James 4:8

This is how we know that we abide in him
and he in us: he has given us his Spirit.

1 John 4:13

For the Spirit
God gave us
does not make us
timid,
but gives us
power,
love and
self-discipline.

2 Timothy 1:7

Wait for the LORD; be strong,
and let your heart take courage;
wait for the LORD!

Psalm 27:14

He who began a good work in you will carry it on to completion.

Philippians 1:6

O God, thou art my God; early will I
seek thee: my soul thirsteth for thee,
my flesh longeth for thee in a dry
and thirsty land, where no water is . . .

Psalm 63:1

Set your minds on things above, not on earthly things.

Colossians 3:2

I will praise the name of God with a song,
and will magnify him with thanksgiving.

Psalm 69:30

Everyone who calls upon the name of the Lord shall be saved.

Acts 2:21